Informing the legislative debate since 1914

U.S. Textile Manufacturing and the Trans-Pacific Partnership Negotiations

Michaela D. Platzer
Specialist in Industrial Organization and Business

August 28, 2014

Congressional Research Service

7-5700

www.crs.gov

R42772

Summary

Textiles are a contentious and unresolved issue in the ongoing Trans-Pacific Partnership (TPP) negotiations to establish a free-trade zone across the Pacific. Because the negotiating parties include Vietnam, a major apparel producer that now mainly sources yarns and fabrics from China and other Asian nations, the agreement has the potential to shift global trading patterns for textiles and demand for U.S. textile exports. Canada and Mexico, both significant regional textile markets for the United States, and Japan, a major manufacturer of high-end textiles and industrial fabrics, are also participants in the negotiations.

U.S. textile manufacturers produce yarn, thread, and fabric for apparel, home furnishings, and various industrial applications. In 2013, the U.S. textile industry generated nearly $57 billion in shipments and directly employed about 230,700 Americans, accounting for approximately 2% of all U.S. factory jobs. More than one-third of U.S. textile production is exported, with the bulk of the exports going to Western Hemisphere nations that are members of the North American Free Trade Agreement (NAFTA), the Dominican Republic-Central America Free Trade Agreement (CAFTA-DR), and the Caribbean Basin Initiative (CBI). These free trade agreements provide that certain exports from member countries may enter the U.S. market duty-free only if they are made from textiles produced in the region. This has encouraged manufacturers in Mexico and Central America to use U.S.-made yarns and fabrics in apparel, home furnishings, and other products. Exports to the NAFTA and CAFTA-DR countries contributed to a U.S. trade surplus of $2.4 billion in yarns and fabrics in 2013.

The TPP has the potential to affect U.S. textile exporters in at least two ways. First, it could enable Asian apparel producers, principally Vietnam, to export clothing to the United States duty-free. This would eliminate much of the advantage now enjoyed by Western Hemisphere apparel producers in the U.S. market and, because Vietnamese manufacturers make little use of U.S.-made textiles, could reduce demand for U.S. textile exports. Second, if the TPP were to allow Western Hemisphere apparel manufacturers to use yarn and fabric made anywhere in the TPP region and still enjoy preferential access to the U.S. market, an enlarged Vietnamese textile industry could, at some future time, compete with U.S. exporters in Mexico and Central America.

Textile industry trade groups have urged the United States to insist on a strict "yarn forward" rule that allows a garment to enter the United States duty-free only if yarn production, fabric production, and cutting and sewing of the finished garment all occur within the TPP region. U.S. negotiators have also proposed that certain textile inputs "not commercially available" in TPP-member countries could be sourced from outside the region, including China. On the other side, retailers and apparel companies with extensive global supply chains want maximum flexibility for sourcing and are less concerned about whether textiles manufactured in the United States are used; they urge textiles and apparel to be treated like other products in any TPP agreement, and they want any apparel cut and sewn within the TPP area, regardless of where the fabric originates, to be eligible for duty-free entry. Members of Congress have voiced their support for both sides.

The TPP seems likely to have less impact on those segments of the U.S. textile industry that do not supply apparel manufacturing. U.S. manufacturers of household and technical textiles appear to be internationally competitive, and it is not evident that lower-wage countries would have comparative advantage in these highly capital-intensive sectors.

Contents

Figures

Tables

Appendixes

Contacts

Introduction

The Trans-Pacific Partnership Agreement (TPP) is a proposed regional free trade agreement (FTA) currently under negotiation among 12 Pacific Rim countries. Initiated under President George W. Bush, the TPP concept has wide bipartisan support.[1] As the negotiations progress, provisions concerning textile trade have become a major point of contention, attracting considerable congressional attention and debate. This report examines the potential implications of a TPP agreement, if one is reached, for the U.S. textile manufacturing industry.

In 2013, the United States exported about $14 billion in yarns and fabrics worldwide. More than half of this output was shipped to Western Hemisphere nations that are members of the North American Free Trade Agreement (NAFTA),[2] the Dominican Republic-Central America Free Trade Agreement (CAFTA-DR),[3] and the Caribbean Basin Initiative (CBI). These FTAs provide that certain exports from member countries may enter the U.S. market duty-free only if they are made from textiles produced in the region. This has encouraged manufacturers in Mexico and Central America to use U.S.-made yarns and fabrics in apparel, home furnishings, and other products. Exports to the NAFTA and CAFTA-DR countries contributed to a U.S. trade surplus of $2.4 billion in yarns and fabrics in 2013.[4]

The TPP marks the first FTA negotiation for the United States initiated since the complete end of quotas on textile and apparel trade.[5] Duty-free access to the U.S. market under TPP could be of considerable benefit to Asian manufacturers, which now face U.S. import duties on textiles and apparel of up to 32%. Textile industry trade groups have warned that, if approved, the TPP could lead to domestic job loss if it results in apparel producers in the Western Hemisphere, which often use U.S.-made textiles, losing U.S. market share to producers in Vietnam and other TPP countries.[6] Aligned against them are retailers and apparel companies that want to be able to import apparel from producers wherever they are located, regardless of whether U.S. textiles are used; they urge full inclusion of textiles and apparel in any TPP agreement and favor preferential access for apparel cut and sewn from fabric made in countries not included in the TPP, such as China.[7]

---

[1] The negotiating partners are Australia, Brunei, Canada, Chile, Japan, Malaysia, Mexico, New Zealand, Peru, Singapore, the United States, and Vietnam. Several other countries have shown interest in joining, including South Korea, a major exporter of textile products to the United States. See CRS Report R42694, *The Trans-Pacific Partnership (TPP) Negotiations and Issues for Congress*, coordinated by Ian F. Fergusson.

[2] NAFTA (approved by Congress in P.L. 103-182) has been in effect since 1994.

[3] The CAFTA-DR free trade agreement (P.L. 109-53) was signed in 2004, first with five Central American countries (Costa Rica, El Salvador, Guatemala, Honduras, and Nicaragua) and then with the Dominican Republic. The United States is also a member. CAFTA-DR was implemented on a rolling basis between 2006 and 2009. CAFTA-DR is discussed in CRS Report R42468, *The Dominican Republic-Central America-United States Free Trade Agreement (CAFTA DR): Developments in Trade and Investment*, by J. F. Hornbeck.

[4] U.S. Commerce Department, Office of Textiles and Apparel (OTEXA), *U.S. textiles and apparel trade balance report*. In 2013, U.S. yarn and fabric imports totaled $11.6 billion.

[5] The Agreement on Textiles and Clothing (ATC) ended in 2005, but China remained subject to textile and apparel quotas through the end of 2008. The other FTAs had been initially concluded and signed by the end of that year.

[6] National Council of Textile Organizations (NCTO), Trade and Jobs, http://www.ncto.org/tradejobs/index.asp.

[7] Trans-Pacific Partnership Apparel Coalition, *TPP Coalition Position Paper*, http://www.tppapparelcoalition.org/uploads/TPP_Apparel_Coalition_One_Pager.pdf.

The U.S. Textile Industry and Its Markets

With nearly $57 billion in industry shipments in 2013, textile manufacturing, which produces yarns and fabrics from raw materials such as cotton and various man-made fibers, is a supplier industry to three industrial sectors.[8] The apparel industry, which transforms textiles into clothing, consumed only 12% of U.S.-manufactured fibers in 2012. About 40% of textile output went into home textiles and floor coverings, while almost half was used in technical textiles such as conveyor belts and automotive floor coverings.[9]

Textile manufacturing occurs largely in highly automated factories, whereas apparel manufacturing is characterized by decentralized, globally dispersed production networks that are coordinated by lead firms that control design, branding, and other activities. Many of the world's largest apparel retailing and marketing firms are headquartered in the United States, but because it typically costs less to manufacture apparel abroad, the United States imports far more clothing than it makes domestically. U.S. apparel shipments totaled more than $13 billion, and apparel manufacturers directly employed 143,600 workers in 2013 (see **Appendix A**).

Unlike textile manufacturers, most U.S.-headquartered apparel firms have limited or no U.S. manufacturing capabilities. Some manufacture through a combination of facilities they own and third-party arrangements, often with foreign factories. Others rely entirely on arrangements with third-party suppliers, mostly in Asia. Large retailers frequently contract directly with apparel sourcing companies, which in turn portion out the production work to independent manufacturers. The United States was responsible for approximately 1% of the $460 billion of global apparel exports in 2013, according to statistics from the World Trade Organization.[10] China, Vietnam, Indonesia, Bangladesh, and Mexico rank as the top apparel suppliers to the United States. Beyond apparel manufacturing, countless other functions related to apparel are done domestically, such as design, branding, and marketing of finished products.[11]

The U.S. home furnishings industry has fared far better against import competition than the apparel industry, mainly because manufacturing of carpets, curtains, and tablecloths is highly automated. For example, the development of larger, faster carpet-tufting machines contributed to a decline in employment at U.S. carpet and rug mills, from 49,000 workers in 2003 to 31,200 in 2013.[12] Shipments from U.S. carpet and rug mills totaled $8.9 billion in 2012.[13] The health of the

---

[8] Shipments data are from U.S. Census Bureau, *Manufacturers' Shipments, Inventories, and Orders (M3) Survey*, http://www.census.gov/manufacturing/m3/. Fabric and yarn manufacturing are classified under North American Industry Classification System (NAICS) code 313. Textile product mills (NAICS 314) include plants making carpets, home linens, tire cord, and other "made-up" articles. Apparel manufacturing is classified under NAICS 315.

[9] "End Use Survey," 2008-2012, *Fiber Organon*, vol. 84, no. 10 (October 2013), p. 188.

[10] World Trade Organization (WTO), International Trade Statistics, 2013, WTO statistics database, updated August 5, 2014, http://stat.wto.org/Home/WSDBHome.aspx?Language=E.

[11] Karina Fernandez-Stark, Stacey Frederick, and Gary Gereffi, *The Apparel Global Value Chain*, Duke University, Center on Globalization, Governance & Competitiveness, November 2011, pp. 7-16, http://www.cggc.duke.edu/pdfs/ 2011-11-11_CGGC_Apparel-Global-Value-Chain.pdf.

[12] Bureau of Labor Statistics (BLS), Quarterly Census of Employment and Wages (QCEW), Carpet and Rug Mills (NAICS 31411), accessed August 5, 2014, http://www.bls.gov/cew/.

[13] U.S. Census Bureau, Annual Survey of Manufactures, 2011 (Carpet and rug mills NAICS 31411).

carpet and rug mills industry is tied in large part to conditions in the domestic housing and commercial building markets, raw material prices, and competition from foreign producers.[14]

The output of technical textile mills is used across various industrial sectors. According to one recent estimate, automotive manufacturers use more than 200,000 tons of textiles for automotive interior fabrics, including upholstery, headliners, and door panels, excluding textiles for carpets, floor mats, tire cords, seat belts, or air bags.[15] The Industrial Fabrics Association International (IFAI) estimated that in 2013 about 160,000 workers in the United States produced fabrics specifically for the technical textile market.[16]

The Textile Manufacturing Process

Textile manufacturing begins with fiber, which can be harvested from natural resources (e.g., cotton, wool, silk, or ramie), manufactured from cellulosic materials (e.g., rayon or acetate), or made of man-made synthetic materials (e.g., polyester, nylon, or acrylic). After the raw fibers are shipped from the farm or the chemical plant, they pass through four main stages of processing (see **Figure 1**):

- yarn production, in which fiber is spun into filament or yarn;

- fabric production, which can take place at very small mills or large textile mill operations, and involves primarily either weaving or knitting;

- finishing, which prepares the textiles for further use by processes such as bleaching, printing, dyeing, and mechanical or wet finishing; and,

- fabrication, where the finished cloth is converted into apparel, household, or industrial products.

---

[14] Zeeshan Haider, "Carpet Mills in the US – New foundations: Industry operators will benefit from a renewed renovation market," IBISWorld Industry Report 31411, August 2014, pp. 7-11.

[15] Robert Reichard, "Textiles 2013: The Turnaround Continues," *Textile World*, September 2013.

[16] Email exchange with Jeffrey Rasmussen, market research manager, Industrial Fabrics Association International (IFAI), August 20, 2014.

Figure 1. Major Products of the Fiber, Textile, and Apparel Industries

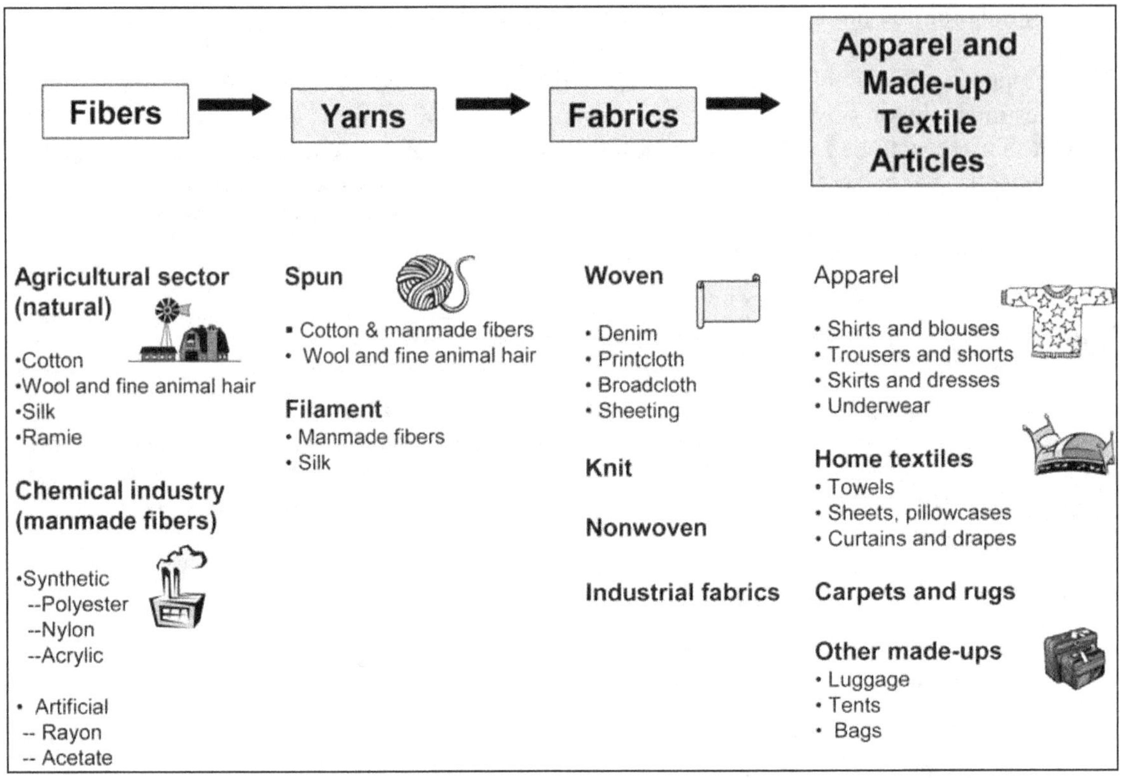

Source: International Trade Commission, *Textiles and Apparel: Assessment of the Competitiveness of Certain Foreign Suppliers to the U.S. Market*, Volume 1, Investigation No. 332-448, Publication 3671, Figure 1-1, January 2004.

Worldwide, in 2013, the textile industry produced 86.6 million metric tons of textiles. Man-made fibers accounted for more than two-thirds of total production, compared to the share of natural to man-made fibers at about half in the 1990s.[17] Most of the global growth in man-made textile manufacturing has taken place in China, which by 2013 accounted for about two-thirds of total production. The United States was responsible for 5% of global production of man-made fibers in 2013. No other country produced more than 4% of the global total in 2013.[18]

Cotton is the most important natural fiber.[19] In the 2013-2014 marketing year, China ranked as the world's largest producer of cotton at 7 million metric tons, followed by India and the United States.[20] Other large cotton producers include Pakistan, Brazil, Uzbekistan, and Turkey. Many of the leading cotton producers are also leading mill users of raw cotton. The top four consumers of cotton are China, India, Pakistan, and Turkey, which together account for more than two-thirds of world consumption. Consumption of cotton by U.S. textile mills peaked in 1997.[21] Since then,

---

[17] Industrievereinigung Chemiefaser e.V., *World-production of Man-Made Fibers, Wool, and, Cotton, Production Since 1975*, https://www.ivc-ev.de/live/index.php?page_id=87.

[18] Andreas Engelhardt, *The Fiber Year 2014*, World Survey on Textiles & Nonwovens, May 2014, p. 188. *Fiber Year 2014* shows global production of man-made fibers in millions of metric tons.

[19] Of total fiber production in 2013, cotton represented around 30% and wool 1%.

[20] U.S. Department of Agriculture, *Cotton: World Markets and Trade*, August 2014, p. 6, http://apps fas.usda.gov/psdonline/circulars/cotton.pdf.

[21] Daryll E. Ray and Harwood D. Schaffer, *Most U.S. Cotton Production Traditionally Went to Domestic Mills, Now it Goes Abroad*, Agricultural Policy Analysis Center, University of Tennessee, Knoxville, September 27, 2013, (continued...)

due to the decrease in domestic textile production caused by competition from imported textile and apparel products, U.S. mill use of cotton has dropped about 70%.[22] As for other natural fibers, two TPP negotiating partners, Australia and New Zealand, are among the world's leading wool-growing nations.[23] Vietnam is a top 10 producer of silk, but accounts for only a small portion of global production. China and India are the world's two largest silk producers.[24]

Domestic Textile Production

U.S. textile output has not recovered from the severe downturn in 2008 and 2009. Production at textile mills remains about 25% below the 2007 level, and production at textile product mills is approximately 30% less than in 2007.[25] The value of shipments totaled nearly $57 billion in 2013, a 5% increase over 2012. This amounted to 1% of total U.S. manufacturing shipments (see **Appendix A**).

According to government data, there were 2,555 fewer establishments manufacturing textiles in 2012 than in 2003.[26] **Appendix B** provides an overview of selected U.S.-headquartered textile manufacturers. Although the National Council of Textile Organization (NCTO) reported in recent congressional testimony that "the textile industry has invested over $3 billion in new technologies, machinery, and manufacturing facilities since 2010,"[27] the most recent data, for 2012, show a continued drop in the number of establishments producing textiles.

Domestic textile manufacturers have invested heavily in technology to reduce operating costs. For example, modern industrial looms incorporate air-jets to weave at speeds of 2,000 picks per minute (compared with 200 picks in 1980, which at the time was considered fast).[28] Some modern textile mills have become almost completely automated, churning out thousands of square yards every hour with as few as 10 or 20 employees. According to the U.S. Census Bureau, the U.S. textile industry invested $18.9 billion in new plants and equipment between 2001 and 2012.[29] Since then, several manufacturers, including Gildan Activewear, Parkdale Mills, Zagis USA, and

---

(...continued)

http://agpolicy.org/weekcol/687.html.

[22] James Johnson, Stephen MacDonald, and Leslie Meyer, et al., *The World and United States Cotton Outlook*, U.S. Department of Agriculture, Agricultural Outlook Forum 2014, February 21, 2014, pp. 8-9, http://www.thecottonschool.com/Agricultural%20%20Outlook%20Forum%202014-The%20U.S.%20and%20World%20Cotton%20Outlook%202.21.14.pdf.

[23] *Fiber Year 2014* reports seven countries (Australia, China, New Zealand, India, South Africa, Argentina, Uruguay, and the United Kingdom) account for more than half of global wool output, p. 52.

[24] Food and Agricultural Organization (FAO), Statistical Division, http://faostat fao.org/site/339/default.aspx.

[25] Federal Reserve Board, Release G. 17, Industrial Production and Capacity Utilization, for NAICS 313 and 314.

[26] U.S. Census Bureau, *County Business Patterns*, data for NAICS 313 and 314..

[27] NCTO, Statement of the National Council of Textile Organizations before the United States House Committee on Small Business, Subcommittee on Economic Growth, Tax and Capital Access, July 9, 2013, p. 5, http://www ncto.org/newsroom/Testimony20130709--SmythMcKissick--AliceMfgFINAL.pdf.

[28] John Varrasi, *Transforming the Textile Industry*, ASME, April 2012, https://www.asme.org/engineering-topics/articles/manufacturing-processing/transforming-the-textile-industry.

[29] U.S. Census Bureau, *Annual Capital Expenditures Survey*, 2012 data, March 12, 2014, https://www.census.gov/econ/aces/.

Keer, have announced plans to increase U.S. production of yarns, nonwoven and technical fabrics, and other types of textiles by building new textile plants or expanding current facilities.[30]

Because yarn and fabric production are capital- and scale-intensive, they demand higher worker skills than apparel production. As a consequence, the textile industry has been less prone to relocation to lower-wage countries than apparel manufacturing. Significant production remains in the United States, Japan, and South Korea, where skilled labor is available and manufacturers can raise the capital to finance weaving mills costing an estimated $12 million to $25 million and spinning mills costing $50 million to $70 million.[31]

Among all U.S. manufacturing industries, textiles rank near the top in productivity increases. This can be attributed both to automation and to the closure of less efficient mills. While imports of textiles and apparel undoubtedly have contributed to lower industry employment, over the past decade more than 200,000 textile manufacturing jobs have been lost due to automation, according to private estimates.[32]

At the end of 2013, the domestic textile industry employed about 230,700 workers, accounting for fewer than 2% of the nearly 12 million domestic factory jobs (see **Appendix A**). Average annual pay was $39,000 in 2013, far below the average of $61,096 for all manufacturing. **Figure 2** shows employment has declined by two-thirds since 1990.[33] Over time, employment has fallen most rapidly during economic downturns, but has failed to return to prerecession levels during the ensuing recoveries. The Bureau of Labor Statistics predicts overall textile manufacturing employment will shrink to around 180,000 by 2022.[34]

Domestic textile production is primarily located in the southeastern states and in California, although every state has some textile manufacturing. In 2013, more than one-third of all textile jobs were located in Georgia and North Carolina. **Appendix C** compares textile employment in the top 10 states, which accounted for more than two-thirds of all textile jobs, in 2003 and 2013.

---

[30] "U.S. Textiles: Investments Abound," *Textile World*, March 2014, http://www.textileworld.com/Issues/2014/March-April/Features/U.S._Textiles-Investments_Abound.

[31] Nathan Associates, *Bringing Hope to Haiti*'s Apparel Industry, World Bank, November 2009, p. 6.

[32] Robert Reichard, "Textiles 2013: The Turnaround Continues," *Textile World*, January/February 2013, http://www.textileworld.com/Articles/2013/January/January_February_issue/Textiles_2013.html.

[33] BLS, Quarterly Census of Employment and Wages (QCEW), accessed August 5, 2014, at http://www.bls.gov/cew/.

[34] Richard Henderson, "Industry Employment and Output Projections to 2022," *Monthly Labor Review*, December 2013.

Figure 2. Textile Manufacturing Employment

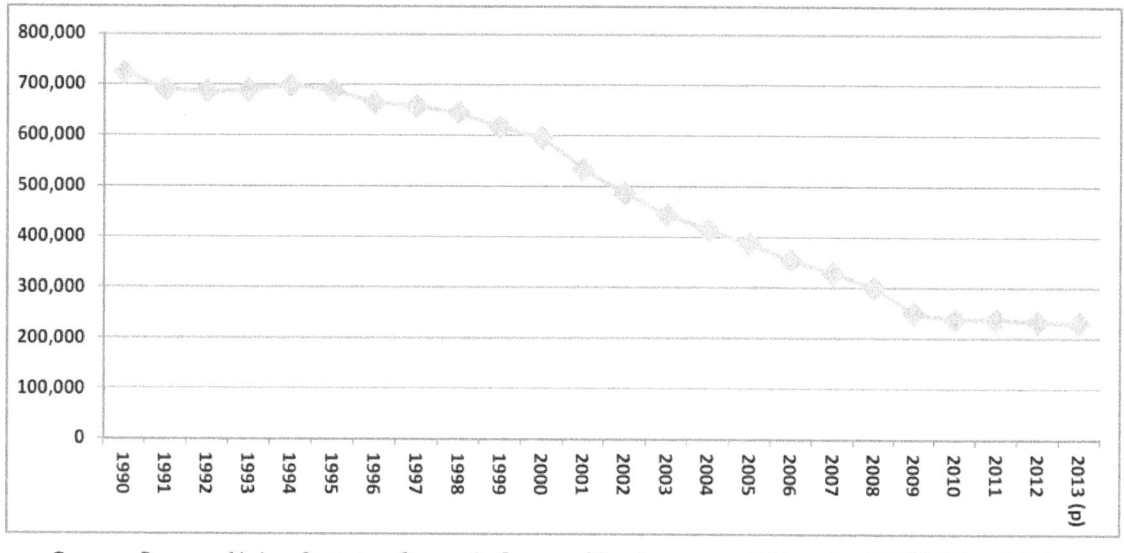

Source: Bureau of Labor Statistics, Quarterly Census of Employment and Wages for NAICS 313 and 314.

In related apparel manufacturing, employment has shrunk every year for more than two decades, resulting in 800,000 fewer U.S. apparel manufacturing jobs in 2013 than in 1990 as clothing manufacturers have transferred much of their production abroad. Some industry analysts assert that a "Made in the USA" label is being sought by more consumers, and a small and select group of apparel retailers, such as Brooks Brothers, has responded by resuming a portion of their manufacturing in the United States.[35] In aggregate, however, apparel work has continued to diminish. Industry employment in 2013 dropped to nearly 144,000, representing a reduction of more than 55,000 jobs since 2008.[36]

Global Textile Trade Shifts

For more than 40 years, developed countries, including the United States and the European Union, sought to protect their textile and apparel sectors from developing countries' exports through two multilateral agreements, the Multi-Fiber Arrangement (MFA) and the Agreement on Textiles and Clothing (ATC). Quotas on imports from more than 70 countries limited the quantities of textiles (such as cotton yarns and synthetic fabrics) and particular garments (such as t-shirts and sweaters) that could enter the United States and the European Union each year. This system made it necessary for buyers of textile and apparel products to source from countries for which quotas for particular products were available. This spread manufacturing to an ever-increasing number of countries, instead of concentrating it where production was cheapest.

The expiry of the ATC on January 1, 2005, eliminated all textile and apparel quotas for members of the World Trade Organization (WTO). Since then, buyers have been able to source from any WTO member country, subject only to tariffs. However, U.S. tariffs on textile and apparel imports vary considerably from country to country, governed by bilateral and regional arrangements

---

[35] Plunkett Research, *Guide to the Apparel and Textile Industry*, May 2, 2014, p. 5.

[36] BLS QCEW program, accessed August 11, 2014, http://www.bls.gov/cew/.

discussed in greater detail below. The average U.S. tariff rate in 2012 was 7.9% for textiles and 11.4% for clothing, but rates on particular products could be as high as 32% (see **Appendix D**).[37]

According to the WTO, China was by far the world's largest exporter of textiles in 2013, with about a 35% global market share at $107 billion. China has been a major force in textiles for decades, but its export growth accelerated following its 2001 accession to the WTO and the expiration of the ATC. Now, more than 50,000 textile mills operate in China.[38] China's textile exports have risen more than 550%, from $16 billion, since 2000 (**Figure 3**). The European Union and India ranked as the world's second- and third-largest exporters of textiles in 2013. The European Union (based on extra-EU imports), the United States, China, Vietnam, and Hong Kong were the world's top five importers of textiles in 2013.[39]

Figure 3. Top Global Textile Exporters

In Billions of U.S. Dollars

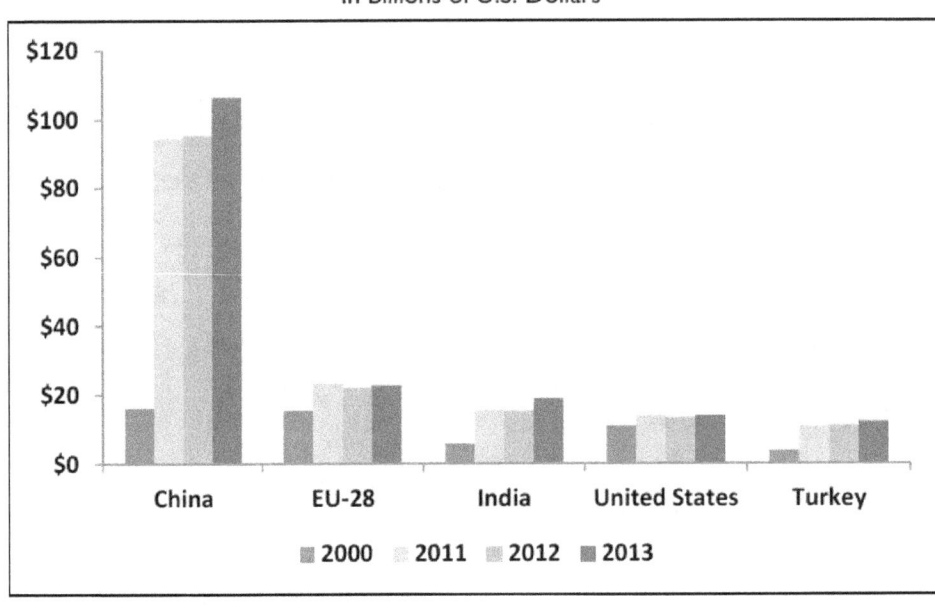

Source: WTO, International Trade Statistics, 2013 Statistics Database.

Notes: Figures for the EU-28 only include exports to the rest of the world. If internal trade were included, EU countries' combined textile exports totaled $72.2 billion in 2013, second to China's $107 billion.

Apparel trade is more diversified than textile trade, as many nations have been able to develop export-oriented apparel industries on the basis of imported fabrics, without having large domestic textile production. China, the EU-28, Bangladesh, Hong Kong, and Vietnam ranked as the top clothing exporters in 2013. Central America, the Caribbean, and Africa, and countries throughout Asia, including Malaysia, also export large quantities of apparel.[40]

---

[37] WTO, *World Tariff Profiles 2013*, p. 170, http://www.wto.org/english/res_e/booksp_e/tariff_profiles13_e.pdf.

[38] Linda Greer, Susan Egan Keane, and Zixin Lin, *NRDC's Ten Best Practices for Textile Mills to Save Money and Reduce Pollution*, National Resources Defense Council (NRDC), February 2010, p. 5, http://www.nrdc.org/international/cleanbydesign/files/rsifullguide.pdf.

[39] WTO, International Trade Statistics, 2013, WTO statistics database, updated August 5, 2014, http://stat.wto.org/Home/WSDBHome.aspx?Language=E.

[40] According to merchandise trade statistics from the WTO, in 2013, Malaysia, Pakistan, Mexico, Thailand, Honduras, (continued...)

U.S. Trade in Textile Products

In 2013, approximately one-third of U.S. textile production was exported, with a value of $17.8 billion (see **Table 1**). The United States has posted a modest trade surplus in fabrics and yarns for 19 years, but when made-up textile articles (e.g., sheets and towels) are included, the United States ran a textile trade deficit of $17.2 billion in 2013. Import penetration—the share of U.S. demand met by textile imports—reached 37% in 2013, from 31% in 2008 (see **Appendix A**).

Table 1. U.S. Exports of Textile Mill Products to the World

In Millions of U.S. Dollars, by Selected Years

	Fabric	Yarn	Made-Up Articles[a]	Textile Mill Products Total	Fabric and Yarn Total
1990	$2,903	$2,141	$1,232	$6,276	$5,044
1995	$4,770	$2,818	$1,727	$9,315	$7,588
2000	$7,420	$3,130	$2,258	$12,808	$10,550
2005	$8,810	$3,271	$2,586	$14,667	$12,081
2006	$8,759	$3,701	$2,777	$15,237	$12,460
2007	$8,375	$3,932	$2,982	$15,289	$12,307
2008	$8,146	$4,259	$3,148	$15,553	$12,406
2009	$6,354	$3,455	$2,832	$12,642	$9,810
2010	$7,637	$4,444	$3,152	$15,233	$12,081
2011	$8,257	$5,623	$3,398	$17,278	$13,880
2012	$8,495	$5,068	$3,568	$17,131	$13,563
2013	$8,865	$5,177	$3,760	$17,802	$14,042

Source: U.S. Department of Commerce. Office of Textiles and Apparel Trade (OTEXA).

Note: Export Market Report, accessed August 11, 2014.

a. Made-up articles include home furnishings and other consumer goods such as towels, tablecloths, and bedsheets.

As **Table 2** shows, the majority of yarns and fabrics exported from the United States are sold to NAFTA and CAFTA-DR countries. U.S. exports are often more expensive than those from other countries. Despite this cost differential, apparel producers in the NAFTA, CAFTA-DR, and CBI countries use U.S.-made textiles in products that are exported to the United States because the goods are free of U.S. tariffs. Mexico is the U.S. textile industry's largest foreign market, with exports of $4.2 billion in 2013. However, textile exports to Mexico have shrunk as a share of total U.S. yarn and fabric exports compared with 2000, as rising labor costs have made it a less attractive place to manufacture apparel and production has shifted to Central America. Less than $400 million of U.S.-made yarns and fabrics was exported to other prospective TPP member countries such as Japan, Malaysia, and Vietnam in 2013.

(...continued)

Morocco, Tunisia, Panama, and El Salvador ranked among the world's 25 largest apparel exporting countries by value.

Table 2. U.S. Yarn and Fabric Exports, by Countries or Region

In Millions of U.S. Dollars, by Selected Years

	1990	1990 % Share	2000	2000 % Share	2013	2013 % Share
World	$5,044		$10,550		$14,042	
Mexico	$478	9%	$3,726	35%	$4,223	30%
CAFTA-DR[a]	$235	5%	$760	7%	$2,544	18%
Canada	$1,029	20%	$2,328	22%	$1,766	13%
EU-28	$1,372	27%	$1,506	14%	$1,444	10%
China	$163	3%	$210	2%	$1,282	9%
CBI[b]	$109	2%	$74	1%	$75	1%

Source: U.S. Department of Commerce. OTEXA. Accessed August 14, 2014.

Notes:

a. CAFTA-DR consists of Costa Rica, Dominican Republic, El Salvador, Guatemala, Honduras, and Nicaragua.

b. The Caribbean Basin Initiative (CBI) includes Antigua, Aruba, Bahamas, Barbados, Belize, British Virgin Islands, Dominica, Grenada, Guyana, Haiti, Jamaica, Montserrat, Netherlands Antilles, Panama, St. Kitts-Nevis, St. Lucia, St. Vincent/Grenadines, and Trinidad and Tobago.

China, Canada, and the EU-28, with a combined total of $6.2 billion, provided more than half of the yarns and fabrics imported by the United States in 2013. Textile imports are sensitive to the economy: between 2008 and 2009, imports of yarns and fabrics shrank by 24%, but they rose 26% in 2010 and another 14% in 2011 as the economy improved. They increased only 1% in 2012 and again by 1% in 2013.

In the apparel sector, import penetration reached almost 90% of U.S. demand in 2013, up from 83% in 2008 (see **Appendix A**). The U.S. trade deficit in apparel products was $77 billion in 2013.[41] Nearly 40% of imported apparel came from China. Vietnam, a fast-growing source of apparel for the U.S. market, furnished 10% of imports, and Mexico accounted for 5%, but the other TPP participants shipped only small quantities of apparel to the United States. Almost all U.S. apparel imports from Central America, the Caribbean, Mexico, and Canada are made with textiles produced in the United States. Collectively, they accounted for 16% of U.S. apparel imports in 2013, down from a third in 2000.

Sourcing in the Western Hemisphere

Central America, Mexico, and the Caribbean have limited textile production, but ample cut, make, and trim apparel assembly capacity, or CMT production as it is known in the industry. CMT is a low-value-added production system, whereby a manufacturer produces garments for a customer by cutting fabric provided by the customer, sewing the cut fabric, trimming the thread, and packaging the garments according to the customer's specifications. Canada's higher-value-added textile sector differs substantially from the CMT operations in Latin America. U.S. textile exports to Canada, mainly specialty and industrial fabrics, totaled $1.8 billion in 2013.

---

[41] OTEXA Textile and Apparel Trade Balance Report, accessed August 11, 2014, http://otexa.ita.doc.gov/tbrbal.htm.

In Central America, virtually all fibers are imported. The Central America-Dominican Republic Apparel and Textile Council reports that the CAFTA-DR region has more than 600 apparel companies. About 90 textile mills produce knit and woven fabrics, man-made fibers, and mixtures.[42] Several U.S. textile manufacturers have manufacturing capabilities in Central America, as have companies from South Korea, Taiwan, and China.

Mexico is home to approximately 30 mills producing yarns and knitted and woven fabrics.[43] U.S.-based firms produce significant amounts of denim there.[44] Among the regional apparel suppliers that have free-trade agreements with the United States, Mexico is the only significant producer of fabric and the only significant source of yarn.

Mexico's apparel industry relies almost entirely on the U.S. market for exports. Its cut and assembly operations often use U.S.-made fabrics to produce basic garments such as denim jeans and T-shirts, which are then exported to the United States. Mexico ranked as the largest yarn and fabric market for the United States in 2013 at $4.2 billion, with significant purchases of impregnated fabrics, felt and specialty yarns, and man-made fibers and filaments (see **Figure 4**). Competition from countries with lower wages appears to be reducing the competitiveness of Mexican apparel. U.S. clothing imports from Mexico dropped to $3.8 billion in 2013, from $6.3 billion in 2005.[45]

For U.S. textile exporters, Honduras, the Dominican Republic, El Salvador, and Guatemala represent the biggest yarn and fabric markets in the CAFTA-DR region.[46] At $1.3 billion, Honduras was the largest of the four in 2013, absorbing 9% of total U.S. yarn and fabric exports. Cotton (yarn/woven fabric), man-made fibers, and man-made filaments, which are used to make basic apparel such as T-shirts, socks, and underwear, are among the top export categories from the United States to Honduras.[47] The Dominican Republic, El Salvador, and Guatemala are also major assemblers of basic apparel for the U.S. market.

Nicaragua benefits from a unique feature of the CAFTA-DR agreement: the inclusion of a tariff preference level (TPL) provision. The TPL allows U.S. trade preferences for Nicaraguan apparel that uses non-U.S. or non-CAFTA yarns and fabrics in limited amounts.[48] Even with the TPL, which is scheduled to expire at the end of 2014,[49] U.S. exports of yarns and fabrics to Nicaragua

---

[42] Central America-Dominican Republic Apparel and Textile Council based on data from International Development Systems (IDS), http://www.apparelcentralamericadr.com/cecatec-dr/.

[43] Gary Gereffi and Jennifer Bair, *Strengthening Nicaragua's Position in the Textile-Apparel Value Chain: Upgrading in the Context of the CAFTA-DR Region*, Center on Globalization, Governance & Competitiveness, December 20, 2010, Table 10, p. 43, http://www.cggc.duke.edu/pdfs/2010-12-20_Gereffi_Bair_Nicaragua-apparel-report.pdf.

[44] Greg Houser, "The Return of Cone Mills Denim," *Oxford American*, June 11, 2014, http://www.oxfordamerican.org/articles/2014/jun/11/return-cone-mills-denim/.

[45] OTEXA, Textile and Apparel Trade Balance Report, accessed August 12, 2014, http://otexa.ita.doc.gov/msrpoint.htm.

[46] Honduras has been the largest yarn export market for the United States since 2007, with exports of nearly $1.0 billion in 2013, or about one-fifth of all U.S. yarn exports. U.S. exports of fabrics to Honduras totaled $328 million last year. In recent years, Honduras has become stronger in knit fabrics due to investments by manufacturers such as Parkdale, VF Corporation, and Premier Narrow Fabrics.

[47] OTEXA, *Going Global*, Export Guide for Textiles and Apparel, August 2013, pp. 8.

[48] The Nicaraguan TPL allows some foreign components, including from Asian countries like China and Vietnam, to be sent to CAFTA countries for assembly and then exported duty-free to the United States.

[49] Senator Diane Feinstein introduced the Nicaraguan Tariff Preference Level Extension Act of 2013 (S. 1136) to extend the TPL for Nicaragua through 2024. Separately, Senator Kay Hagan introduced the Extending Incentives for (continued...)

---

remain relatively tiny at less than $100 million in 2013.[50] Costa Rica also has a TPL provision applicable to wool and certain women's swimwear.[51]

Figure 4. U.S. Fabric and Yarn Exports to the Western Hemisphere
In Billions of U.S. Dollars

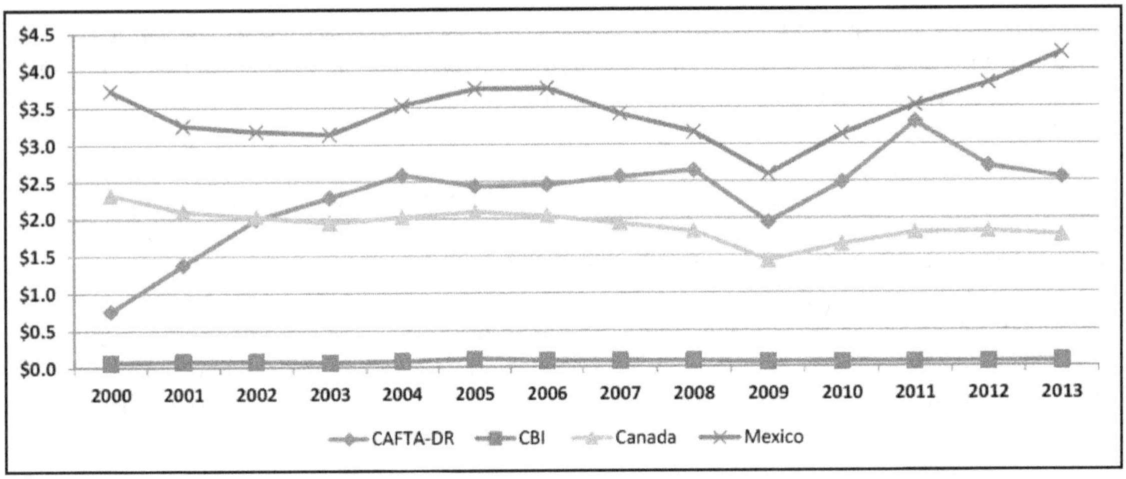

Source: OTEXA, International Trade Administration, U.S. Department of Commerce.

Notes: These figures only cover yarn and fabric exports. They exclude made-up textiles.

Apparel manufacturers in the Caribbean region also have preferential access to the U.S. market under the Caribbean Basin Initiative (CBI), now called the Caribbean Basin Trade Preference Act (CBTPA) program. Because production of yarn and fabric in the Caribbean is extremely limited, the region's cut and assembly factories mostly rely on U.S.-made fabrics and yarns, with U.S. exports totaling $75 million in 2013. Most textile production in the Caribbean is located in the Dominican Republic (also a CAFTA member).[52] Other Caribbean countries such as Haiti have no domestic textile industries, but use U.S.-made textiles to produce apparel for the U.S. market.

U.S. retailers buy most of their garments from Asia and tend to use Western Hemisphere producers for quick replenishment, especially if time is a critical factor. The major products sourced within the region are basic, low-value knitwear garments, such as shirts, pants, underwear, and nightwear, with a focus on men's and boys' wear. U.S. imports of industrial fabrics from the CAFTA-DR region are relatively minimal at $1.5 million in 2013.[53]

Apparel producers in the Western Hemisphere have two main comparative advantages in serving the U.S. market. One is geographic proximity, which confers lower transportation costs and faster

---

(...continued)
Exporting American Textiles Act of 2013 (S. 1883), which would extend the Nicaragua TPL for 10 years only for woven trousers and shorts, subject to an earned import allowance program.

[50] Jon Fee, *TPP, Nicaragua TPL and What's in Store*, Alston& Bird LLP, May 5, 2014, pp. 22-27.

[51] Costa Rica, the last to implement CAFTA-DR, has increasingly ceded apparel manufacturing to other Central American countries shifting to higher value-added goods, including electronics, and other industries such as tourism.

[52] Fair Labor Association, *The Apparel Industry in the Dominican Republic after the MFA*, Report and Recommendations of an FLA Mission, p. 12, June 2007.

[53] Various types of technical fabrics are found in OTEXA Category 229 (special purpose fabrics).

delivery; transit times from the CAFTA-DR region to a U.S. port range from two to seven days,[54] rather than about two weeks to a month from Asia.[55] The other advantage is duty-free access for apparel manufactured from U.S. textiles. For example, manufacturers of cotton T-shirts or cotton twill trousers can avoid a 16.5% import duty if U.S. inputs are used.[56]

On the other side of the ledger, Mexico, Central America, and the Caribbean Basin have much higher wage rates than some Asian apparel suppliers, such as Vietnam, Cambodia, and Bangladesh. A 2010 study, for example, found the apparel industry's average hourly cost of labor to be $2.06 in Mexico, but only $0.51 in Vietnam.[57]

Tariff preferences appear to be important in keeping apparel producers in the Western Hemisphere competitive in the U.S. market, and thereby preserving export markets for U.S.-made textiles. A TPP agreement, if one is reached, has the potential to upset this situation. If apparel produced in Asian TPP countries gains duty-free access to the U.S. market, it could displace apparel manufactured with U.S. fabric in the Western Hemisphere, adversely affecting U.S. textile exports. Also, should Vietnam develop a larger textile industry, U.S. textile exports could be hurt if the TPP were to allow Western Hemisphere apparel producers to use textiles made in any TPP member country and still enjoy duty-free access to the U.S. market.

TPP and Sourcing from Vietnam

Vietnam, which had a negligible garment manufacturing sector a decade ago, is now the second-largest exporter of garments to the United States, behind China.[58] As shown in **Figure 5**, apparel imports to the United States from China, which is not involved in the TPP negotiations and is unlikely to enter the TPP in the near future, reached more than $31 billion in 2013. U.S. apparel imports from Vietnam, although far smaller, have grown even faster, rising from near zero in 2000 to $8.2 billion in 2013. U.S. imports of clothing from Vietnam in 2013 were more than twice the value of apparel imports from Mexico. U.S. imports of technical fabrics from Vietnam have also expanded in recent years, totaling $186 million in 2013, but are still far smaller than apparel imports.[59] Among the Asian and Pacific countries in the TPP, Vietnam is the only one with significant textile and apparel trade with the United States.

---

[54] Transit times obtained from Maersk Line, http://www.maerskline.com, September 2012.

[55] Department of Commerce, Assess Costs Everywhere, http://acetool.commerce.gov/shipping.

[56] The 2013 Normal Trade Relations (NTR) duty rate for cotton T-shirts (HTS 6109.10.00) is 16.5% and men's woven cotton pants (HTS 6203.42.40) is 16.6% at an ad valorem (percent of value) rate. Tariff savings for other products can be found on the USITC website at http://dataweb.usitc.gov/scripts/tariff_current.asp.

[57] O'Rourke Group Partners, *Benchmarking the Competitiveness of Nicaragua's Apparel Industry*, Carana Corporation, April 2011, pp. 19-21, http://www.mayorganet.com/downloads/nicaraguanapparel.pdf.

[58] Vietnam became a WTO member in 2007, entitling it to lower U.S. tariffs. In 2012, Vietnam's applied duties were 9.6% for textiles and 19.8% for apparel.

[59] Vietnam accounted for 8% of the $2.3 billion of industrial fabrics (HS 59) imported into the United States in 2013. Canada was the largest supplier at $439 million, accounting for about one-fifth of imports, followed by China and Mexico.

Figure 5. U.S. Apparel Imports

In Billions of U.S. Dollars, by Selected Countries

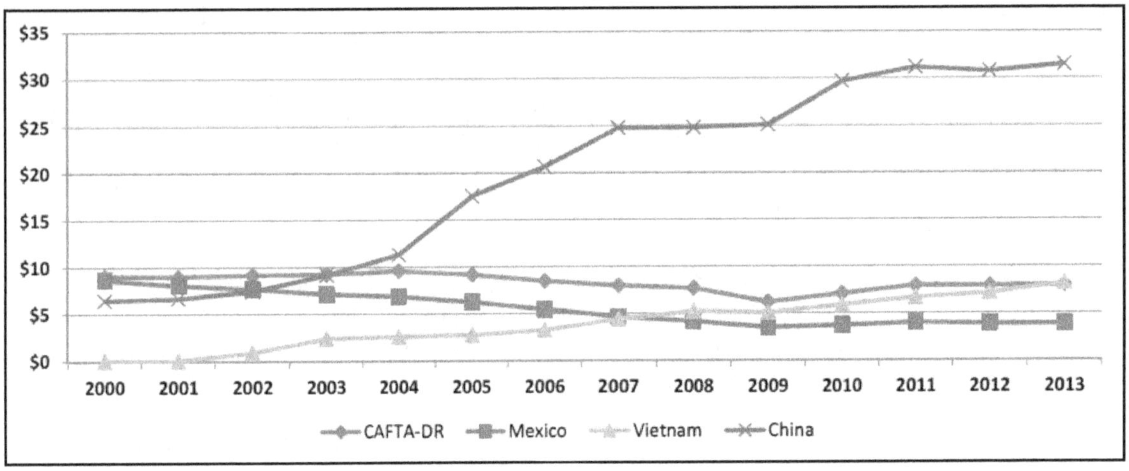

Source: OTEXA.

Generally, the main competitors to Vietnam in the U.S. clothing market are not Mexico and the CAFTA-DR nations, but China and other Asian nations. Vietnam tends to sell fewer basic apparel products (e.g., T-shirts and trousers) and more shirts, suits, and overcoats in the United States than do Western Hemisphere trading partners. For example, in 2013, Vietnam provided 18% of total U.S. imports of women's or girls' blouses, shirts, and suits, both knitted and woven.[60]

Vietnam's apparel sector buys the majority of its yarns and fabrics regionally, from China and other Asian suppliers such as South Korea and Taiwan, and purchases only a limited amount from the United States.[61] The country does have a growing textile industry, comprising 145 spinning mills, 401 weaving mills, 105 knitting mills, 94 dyeing and finishing mills, and 7 non-woven mills.[62] However, Vietnam has yet to develop a broad textile supply base and imports are estimated to account for the overwhelming majority of the fibers, fabrics, and yarns required by its apparel industry. One press report mentions that Vietnamese garment producers obtain only about 12%-13% of fabrics and other input materials, including raw materials such as cotton, from local textile manufacturers.[63]

The Vietnam National Textile and Garment Group, or Vinatex, is Vietnam's largest textile and garment producer.[64] Vinatex, partially state owned,[65] is one of several groups that are investing to

---

[60] Analysis based on Global Trade Atlas data, HTS 6104 (women's or girls' suits and ensembles) and HTS 6106 (women's or girls' blouses and shirts).

[61] The Trans-Pacific Partnership Apparel Coalition claims more than half of yarn used in Vietnam comes from Taiwan and China. See *Common Myths about the Trans-Pacific Partnership and Yarn Forward Rule of Origin*, March 2013, p. 1, http://www.tppapparelcoalition.org/uploads/030113TPPMythFactSheet.pdf.

[62] Gladys Lopez-Acevedo and Raymond Robertson, Sewing Success? (Washington, DC: World Bank 2012), p. 478. Vietnam's textile industry developed in the 1980s in the framework of bilateral economic cooperation agreements with other Communist countries, but many of these plants were abandoned in the 1990s. In more recent years, Vietnam has begun to rebuild its textile industry, and foreign manufacturers from Japan, South Korea, Taiwan, and China, and other countries, are increasing their investments in Vietnam's yarn and fabric sector.

[63] Sara C. Thomasson, "Vietnam on the Move," *Textile World Asia*, June 2014, http://www.textileworldasia.com/Issues/2014/April-May-June/Features/Vietnam_On_The_Move.

[64] European Commission, *2011 Report on Vietnam*, May 2011, pp. 15-17, http://eeas.europa.eu/delegations/vietnam/documents/eu_vietnam/greenbook_11_en.pdf.

---

increase fiber and fabric production in Vietnam. In 2013, Vinatex's exports were valued at $2.95 billion, with the aim of reaching $5 billion by 2016.[66] Nationally, Vietnam's Ministry of Trade and Industry has set a development strategy for the textile and garment sector, aiming to increase fabric production to 2 million metric tons by 2020.[67] Fiber production is targeted to increase to 500,000 metric tons in 2015 and 650,000 metric tons by 2020. Fiber factories to help reduce Vietnam's dependence on imported materials include a joint venture between Vinatex and PetroVietnam Petrochemical & Textile Fiber Joint Stock Company to build a polyester fiber plant at Dinh Vu.[68] Additional Vinatex projects include a new textile complex for spinning, weaving, sewing, dyeing, and finishing, and a partnership with two Chinese companies to build a large garment and textile industrial park in Vietnam.[69] Investments in chemical plants to generate the basic feedstocks required for the production of synthetic fabrics may follow.

According to *Vietnam Investment Review*, "a new wave of foreign investments in the spinning, weaving, and dyeing sectors has been kicked off, since investors can see the profits they can gain from the TPP."[70] According to one estimate, foreign manufacturers have invested more than $1 billion in Vietnam's textile and apparel sector in anticipation of a TPP agreement.[71] For example, major Chinese companies, such as Texhong and Pacific Textile, are opening new textile plants in Vietnam, partly attracted by lower labor costs and lower tariffs under a potential TPP.[72] Textile and garment manufacturers based in Japan, Hong Kong, South Korea, Taiwan, Austria, and Australia are also setting up new production or have expanded current production in Vietnam.[73]

Arguably, preferential access to the Vietnamese market under a TPP agreement could result in new business opportunities for U.S. fiber, yarn, and fabric producers. To date, however, Vietnam is not a significant market for U.S. yarn and fabric exporters, importing $59 million of such products in 2013. The United States' main textile-related export to Vietnam is raw cotton: U.S. exports supply about 60% of the cotton used in Vietnamese textile mills.

(...continued)

[65] An overview of Vinatex is available at http://www.vinatex.com. NCTO has identified 11 different subsidy programs by the Vietnamese government to support its domestic textile and apparel sector, including low-cost loans, energy, and research and promotion. See NCTO Fact Sheet, *TPP Negotiations*, p. 3, April 2012, http://www.ncto.org/IndustryIssues/TPP-Fact-Sheet--Apr2012.pdf.

[66] Sara C. Thomasson, "Vietnam on the Move," *Textile World Asia*, June 2014.

[67] WTO, *Trade Policy Review Vietnam*, August 13, 2013, p. 123, http://www.wto.org/english/tratop_e/tpr_e/s287_e.pdf#page=1&zoom=auto,0,842.

[68] Ibid.

[69] "Vinatex Begins Building of Textile Project in Hai Phong," *Fiber2fashion*, December 31, 2013.

[70] Vietnam Investment Review, *TPP May Attract more Foreign Investment Projects in Textiles and Dyeing*, June 19, 2012. http://www.vir.com.vn/news/business/tpp-may-attract-more-foreign-investment-projects-in-textiles-and-dyeing.html.

[71] AmCham Vietnam, *TPP: Another Hong Kong Firm to Investment $200 Million in Vietnam's Textile Industry*, June 2013, http://www.amchamvietnam.com/30441173/tpp-another-hong-kong-firm-to-invest-200-million-in-vietnams-textile-industry/.

[72] Nguyet Thuong, "Chinese Firms Seen Scaling up Investments into Textile Industry," *The Saigon Times*, June 17, 2013.

[73] Foreign companies such as South Korea's Hyosung Corporation (the largest spandex producer in the world) and Kyungbang Group, Japan's Toray International and Mitsui Corporation, Austria's Lenzing, and Australia's Woolmark Company are investing in Vietnam's textile and apparel sector.

Textiles and the TPP Negotiations

Textile and apparel trade is governed by very specific rules. Extensive stipulations for textiles and apparel are included in most of the bilateral and regional FTAs and trade preference programs negotiated by the United States over the past two decades. The key issue is typically rules of origin (ROOs), which specify how much of the content of textile and apparel products must come from the region in order for the products to qualify for duty-free access.[74] ROO requirements for textile and apparel products are usually based on the production process as shown in **Figure 6**.

Figure 6. Major Production Steps for the Textile and Apparel Sector

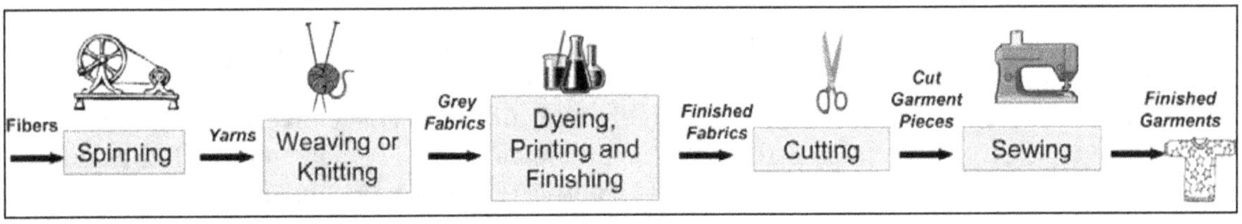

Source: International Trade Commission, *Textiles and Apparel: Assessment of the Competitiveness of Certain Foreign Suppliers to the U.S. Market*, Volume 1, Investigation No. 332-448, Publication 3671, Figure 1-3, January 2004.

Possible rules of origin generally stipulate how much processing must occur within the region if a product is to obtain trade benefits. The major distinctions are:

- **Fiber Forward:** Fiber must be formed in the FTA member territory. Natural fibers such as wool or cotton must be grown in the territory. Man-made fibers must be extruded in the trading area.

- **Yarn Forward:** Fibers may be produced in any country, but each component starting with the yarn used to make the textiles or apparel must be formed within the free trade area. This rule is sometimes called "triple transformation," as it requires that spinning of the yarn or thread, weaving or knitting of the fabric, and assembly of the final product all occur within the region.

- **Fabric Forward:** Producers may use fibers and yarns from any country, but fabric must be knitted or woven in FTA member countries.

- **Cut and Sew:** Only the cutting and sewing of the finished article must occur in FTA member countries, providing maximum flexibility for sourcing.[75]

The United States, most often, has applied the "yarn forward" standard for textiles and apparel, with the notable exceptions of agreements with Jordan and Israel.[76] Most U.S. FTAs also include exceptions allowing limited quantities of fibers, yarns, and fabrics to be sourced from outside the FTA partner countries under certain conditions.[77]

---

[74] CRS Report RL34524, *International Trade: Rules of Origin*, by Vivian C. Jones and Michael F. Martin.

[75] U.S. Customs and Border Protection, *What Every Member of the Trade Community Should Know About: Textile and Apparel Rules of Origin*.

[76] ROOs in the FTAs with Jordan and Israel provide that cutting and sewing, or knitting to shape, fabric finishing, and similar treatment are sufficient to confer origin as long as the value-added requirement of 35% is met.

[77] For example, in NAFTA "fiber forward" applies to man-made fiber sweaters, "fabric forward" to linings for tailored clothing, and "cut and sew" to certain fabrics, including Harris Tweed and velveteen.

Appendix D lists textile and apparel tariff rates of various countries. In general, U.S. tariffs increase with each stage of manufacturing, such that duty rates are usually higher on apparel than on its yarn or fabric inputs. The United States' TPP negotiating partners also tend to maintain steep tariffs. Vietnam's apparel tariffs range from 5% to 20%.

U.S. negotiators have proposed that the TPP agreement incorporate a unified yarn-forward ROO, with perhaps some exemptions for inputs considered to be in short supply, or "not commercially available," in the region[78] to assure that duty-free preferences only benefit countries that are part of the agreement.[79] Press reports indicate that several TPP negotiating countries, including Vietnam, oppose U.S. demands for a "yarn forward" rule.[80] Vietnam publicly supports a "cut and sew" rule that would allow it, and other TPP participants, to enjoy preferential access for apparel that has been cut and sewn from fabric made in China or other countries not included in the TPP.[81]

U.S. domestic interests disagree over what ROOs should be included in any TPP agreement.[82] On one side are fiber, yarn, and fabric manufacturers who want rules that would require more U.S. or TPP content. Organized as the Textile and Apparel Alliance for TPP (TAAT), they have endorsed a basic "yarn forward" rule applicable to all TPP countries.[83] They warn that without such a rule Vietnamese apparel manufacturers could use Chinese textiles, thereby giving Chinese textile manufacturers duty-free access to the U.S. market and undermining U.S. textile production. More than 165 Members of Congress have endorsed TAAT's position, sending a letter in support to the U.S. Trade Representative recommending a yarn-forward rule.[84]

On the other side are U.S. retailers and importers of apparel, many with no domestic manufacturing, along with the National Retail Federation (NRF) and the U.S. Chamber of Commerce. These interests formed the Trans-Pacific Partnership Apparel Coalition, which opposes the "yarn forward" ROO and calls for a "flexible, liberal, 21st century ROO standard" for textiles and apparel. Their preferred rule would require only that the sewing of a garment be done in a TPP country to get duty-free status. This would permit use of yarns and fabrics from China and other countries in garments qualifying for duty-free access to all TPP countries. The TPP Apparel Coalition recommends that apparel qualify for preferential treatment if it meets a regional value content threshold, making it easier to switch sources of supply as fashions and relative costs change.[85] Some Members of Congress support this position, and they asked

---

[78] Items on the "short supply" lists could be sourced either permanently or temporarily from non-TPP countries like China. The proposed lists are confidential, but are said to include more than 200 items. See TPP Apparel Coalition, *TPP Short Supply*, May 2013, http://www.tppapparelcoalition.org/uploads/Short_Supply_Power_Point.pdf.

[79] "ROO, IP, Investment, SOEs Among Groups Meeting at Ottawa TPP Round," *Inside U.S. Trade*, July 10, 2014.

[80] "U.S., Vietnam Signal Flexibilities in TPP Apparel Rule of Origin Fight," *Inside U.S. Trade*, May 24, 2012.

[81] American Apparel & Footwear Association, *Trans-Pacific Partnership (TPP) Workshop*, May 14, 2014, https://www.wewear.org/assets/1/7/TPP_AAFA_Workshop_HCMC_May_2014.pdf.

[82] USTR, *Trans-Pacific Partnership: Summary of U.S. Objectives*, June 2014, http://www.ustr.gov/tpp/Summary-of-US-objectives.

[83] TAAT includes organizations such as the American Fiber Manufacturers Association, National Cotton Council, NCTO, the United States Industrial Fabrics Institute, and overseas groups including the Central American-Dominican Republic Apparel and Textile Council and the Africa Coalition for Trade.

[84] NCTO, "Congress Backs NCTO Letter to USTR Advocating Fair Textile Provisions," press release, July 10, 2013, http://www.ncto.org/newsroom/pr2013-0710--CongressBacksNCTO--LettertoUSTRAdvocatingFairTextileProvisions.pdf.

[85] TPP Apparel Coalition, *Common Myths about the TPP and the Yarn Forward Rule of Origin*, March 2013, p. 6, (continued...)

President Obama in May 2012 to pursue "a flexible general rule of origin for apparel that maximizes the incentive to grow U.S. exports, value, and jobs in the TPP."[86]

Conclusion

Concerns about the health of domestic textile manufacturing have influenced many past trade negotiations, and they now figure prominently in the regional TPP negotiations. For textile manufacturers, the inclusion of a significant apparel producer such as Vietnam in a free trade agreement holds the potential to dramatically shift global trading patterns.

Depending upon its provisions, it is imaginable that a TPP agreement could result in apparel made in Vietnam displacing apparel from the Western Hemisphere in the U.S. market, weakening the export markets now served by U.S. textile producers in Mexico and Central America. An alternative scenario might allow apparel manufacturers in Mexico, a TPP participant, to use textiles made in any TPP country and still enjoy duty-free access to the U.S. market; while no Asian TPP participant currently has the textile production capacity to supply Western Hemisphere producers in this way, it is conceivable that such capacity could be installed in the future.

U.S. textile manufacturing interests have urged U.S. negotiators to insist on a "yarn forward" rule in the TPP. This would require that for apparel, home furnishings, or technical textiles to benefit from duty-free access, they would have to be assembled in a TPP country from fabric manufactured in a TPP country out of yarn produced in a TPP country. Such a rule would severely limit the ability of countries such as Vietnam to use Chinese or Indian yarns and fabrics in apparel, home furnishings, or technical textile products for the U.S. market, although it would not constrain imports if Vietnam were to develop a more fully integrated textile industry. However, a "yarn forward" rule would also affect U.S. apparel consumers and the household textiles and specialty textiles markets, as these products made in TPP countries from yarns and fabrics produced elsewhere would not qualify for duty-free treatment.

Domestic manufacturers of household and technical textiles seem less likely to be immediately affected by any TPP agreement. U.S. manufacturers appear to be internationally competitive in these sectors, and Vietnam's low labor costs will provide little comparative advantage in areas where production is highly automated. In the case of technical textiles, U.S. manufacturers also benefit from proximity to their industrial customers. Domestic technical textile manufacturers point out that Vietnam has been expanding its reach into industrial fabrics and higher-end textiles in recent years, including tire cord and coated fabrics,[87] but Vietnam will probably not be a significant global competitor in the near future.

(...continued)

http://www.tppapparelcoalition.org/uploads/030113TPPMythFactSheet.pdf.

[86] Letter to President Obama from 15 U.S. Senators, May 1, 2012, http://tppapparelcoalition.org/uploads/050112warnertppletter.pdf.

[87] Letter from Ruth A. Stephens, Executive Director, U.S. Industrial Fabrics Institute, to Ambassador Ron Kirk, United States Trade Representative, March 26, 2012.

Appendix A. Textile Industry Overview

	2008	2012	2013	2008-2013
Total U.S. manufacturing employment (all industries)	13,382,697	11,904,945	11,993,947	-10%
Textile mills (NAICS 313)	152,677	117,933	116,805	-23%
Textile product mills (NAICS 314)	147,517	115,462	113,867	-23%
Total textile employment	300,194	233,395	230,672	-23%
Apparel (NAICS 315)	198,678	148,309	143,575	-28%
All textiles and apparel (T&A)	498,872	381,704	374,247	-25%
T&A employment as % of total mfg. employment	4%	3%	3%	
Total value of shipments, in millions of U.S. $				
Total U.S. manufacturing	$5,446,783	$5,724,956	$5,839,450	7%
Textile mills (NAICS 313)	$31,958	$30,779	$31,683	-1%
Textile product mills (NAICS 314)	$26,732	$23,138	$24,889	-7%
Total textile shipments	$58,690	$53,917	$56,572	-4%
Apparel manufacturing (NAICS 315)	$19,148	$13,119	$13,443	-30%
All textiles and Apparel (T&A)	$77,838	$67,036	$70,015	-10%
T&A shipments as % of total mfg. shipments	1.4%	1.2%	1.2%	
U.S. imports for consumption				
Textile mills (NAICS 313)	$6,943	$7,606	$7,850	13%
Textile products (NAICS 314)	$14,985	$17,229	$18,122	21%
Total textile imports	$21,928	$24,835	$25,972	18%
Apparel imports (NAICS 315)	$76,179	$81,192	$84,024	10%
All textiles and apparel	$98,107	$106,027	$109,996	12%
U.S. Exports				
Textile mills (NAICS 313)	$8,209	$8,585	$8,822	7%
Textile products (NAICS 314)	$2,600	$2,865	$2,951	14%
Total textile exports	$10,809	$11,450	$11,773	9%
Apparel exports (NAICS 315)	$3,071	$3,305	$3,279	7%
All textiles and apparel	$13,880	$14,755	$15,052	8%
Apparel imports share of U.S. market	82.6%	89.2%	89.2%	
Textile imports share of U.S. market	31.4%	36.9%	36.7%	

Source: CRS, with data from U.S. Department of Labor, Quarterly Census of Employment and Wages; Census Bureau, Manufacturers' Shipments, Inventories, and Orders, and USITC Dataweb. All data updated in August 2014.

Appendix B. Selected U.S. Textile Manufacturers

Company	Total Employees, 2013	Revenue ($ millions), 2013	Textile Manufacturing Facilities
American & Efird[a]	9,457	$801.9	20 manufacturing facilities worldwide, including the United States, China, and India
International Textile Group[b]	4,800	$624.2	15 manufacturing plants, including seven in the United States, four in Mexico, two in China, and two idled facilities, one in Vietnam and one in Nicaragua.
R. B. Pamplin Corporation[c]	6,205	$443.0	United States, Latin America, the Caribbean, and Asia
Milliken[d]	7,200	$2,910.0	About 40 manufacturing plants in the United States, United Kingdom, Belgium, France, and China
Albany International Group[e]	4,100	$57.4	20 plants globally, five of which manufacture forming fabrics
Polymer Group[f]	4,000	$1,214.9	21 manufacturing and converting facilities in the United States, Europe, Latin America, Canada, Asia
Parkdale Mills[g]	3,000	$237.5	29 manufacturing facilities in the United States, Colombia, and Mexico
Unifi[h]	2,500	$714.0	10 manufacturing operations in United States, Brazil, El Salvador, and Colombia
Lear Corporation[i]	2,600	$198.0	United States, Europe, and a joint venture in China
Mohawk Industries[j]	32,100	$7,348.8	United States, Mexico, and Europe

Source: CRS with information compiled from IBIS World, Hoovers, Plunkett Research, PrivCo, company reports, and websites.

a. American & Efird manufactures industrial sewing thread, embroidery thread, and technical textiles.

b. The International Textile Group (ITG) primary business segments include Burlington Worldwide and the Automotive Safety Group.

c. R.B. Pamplin owns Mount Vernon Mills, a manufacturer of textile, chemical, and related products for the apparel, industrial, institutional, and commercial markets, with 2,700 employees in 2013. Mount Vernon Mills' Georgia integrated denim mill is one of the world's largest denim production facilities.

d. Milliken & Company, a privately held South Carolina-based company, manufactures protective fabrics, specialty fabrics, and industrial textiles, specialty chemicals, performance products, and floor coverings.

e. Albany International produces man-made fibers, mainly for the pulp and paper industry, as well as specialty materials and composites and outdoor clothing, gloves, footwear, sleeping bags, and home furnishings.

f. Polymer is a manufacturer of engineered materials for the hygiene, health care, and textile industries.

g. Parkdale Mills, a privately held North Carolina-based company, manufactures cotton and cotton-polyester blend yarns used in goods such as sheets, towels, underwear, and jeans. It claims to process 60% of U.S. annual cotton consumption, and it is one of the nation's largest textile exporters.

h. Unifi, based in North Carolina, produces multi-filament polyester and nylon textured yarns for apparel, hosiery, furnishings, automotive, industrial, and other uses.

i. Lear Corporation, a supplier of automotive seating and electrical power management systems, purchased Guilford Mills, a maker of automotive and specialty fabrics in 2012.

j. Mohawk, one of the largest carpet makers in the world, produces floor coverings for residential and commercial applications.

Appendix C. Top 10 States in Textile Employment

	2003 Textile Employment	2013 Textile Employment	% Change	# Change
United States	443,891	230,672	-48%	-213,219
Georgia	76,545	44,561	-42%	-31,984
North Carolina	86,003	33,566	-61%	-52,437
South Carolina	49,944	18,340	-63%	-31,604
California	29,601	17,480	-41%	-12,121
Alabama	25,212	10,206	-60%	-15,006
Texas	11,690	8,783	-25%	-2,907
New York	13,523	7,811	-42%	-5,712
Pennsylvania	16,594	7,561	-54%	-9,033
Virginia	17,991	7,199	-60%	-10,792
Tennessee	11,090	6,102	-45%	-4,988
Top 10 States Employment Total	338,193	161,609	-52%	-176,584
Other 40 States plus DC	105,698	69,063	-35%	-36,635
Top 10 States % of Total Employment	76%	70%		

Source: CRS with data compiled from U.S. Bureau of Labor Statistics, Quarterly Census on Employment and Wages, accessed August 2014.

Notes: Textile employment data cover two NAICS codes, 313 and 314. The 50 states and Washington, DC, do not sum to the national total because the national total includes suppressed data and Puerto Rico.

Appendix D. Selected Apparel and Textile Duties

			Ad Valorem[a] Tariff Range			
Country	Yarn	Woven Fabric	Knit Fabric	Non-Woven Fabric	Industrial Fabric	Apparel
FTA Member Countries						
Australia	0%-5%	0%-5%	5%-10%	5%	0-5%	0-10%
Chile	6%	6%	6%	6%	6%	6%
Colombia	5%-15%	5%-10%	5%-10%	5%-10%	5%-10%	15%
Israel	0%-8%	0%-12%	0%-12%	0%-12%	0%-14%	0%-12%
Jordan	0%-20%	0%	0%	0%	0%-20%	0%-20%
Morocco	2.5%	2.5%-25%	10%-25%	2.5%	2.5%-30%	2.5%-30%
Panama	0%-15%	0%-15%	0%	0%	0%-15%	0%-15%
Peru	0%-11%	0%-11%	0%-11%	0%-6%	0%-11%	6%-11%
South Korea	0-8%	2%-13%	10%	8%	8%-10%	8%-13%
CAFTA-DR						
Costa Rica	0%-5%	0%-9%	0%-9%	10%	0%-9%	0%-14%
Dominican Republic	0%	0%-14%	0%-8%	0%	0%-20%	3%-20%
El Salvador	0%-5%	0%-10%	0%-10%	0%	0%-10%	0%-15%
Guatemala	0%	0%-10%	0%-10%	0%	0%-10%	0%-15%
Honduras	0%-5%	0%-10%	0%-10%	0%	0%-10%	0%-15%
Nicaragua	0%-5%	0%-10%	5%-10%	0%	0%-10%	0%-10%
NAFTA[b]						
Mexico	0%-15%	15%	0%-15%	15%	0%-15%	30%
Canada	0%-8%	0%-8%	0%-8%	0%	0%-18%	0%-18%
Other TPP Negotiating Partners						
Brunei	0%	0%	0%	0%	0%-10%	0%
Japan	0%-6.9%	2.5%-12.5%	4%-9.8%	0%-4.3%	2.8%-6.6%	4.4%-12.8%
Malaysia	0%-30%	0%-10%	15%	20%	0%-20%	0%-20%
New Zealand	0%-5%	0%-5%	0%-5%	5%	0%-5%	0%-10%
Vietnam	0%-5%	12%	12%	12%	0%-12%	5%-20%
United States	0%-13.2%	0%-25%	0%-18.5%	0%-12%	0%-14.1%	0%-32%

	Ad Valorem[a] Tariff Range					
Country	**Yarn**	**Woven Fabric**	**Knit Fabric**	**Non-Woven Fabric**	**Industrial Fabric**	**Apparel**
Other Countries						
China	2%-10%	10%-14%	10%-12%	10%	8%-14%	14%-25%
European Union[c]	0%-5%	3%-8%	6.5%-8%	4%	4%-8%	6.3%-12%
Philippines	1%-10%	1%-10%	1%-10%	15%	0%-15%	1%-15%
Thailand	1%-5%	5%-17.5%	5%	5%	1%-30%	10%-30%

Source: CRS with information from U.S. Department of Commerce, Office of Textiles and Apparel (OTEXA).

a.   Ad valorem tariff rates are based on the value of the goods.

b.   Textile and apparel goods manufactured in the United States enter Canada and Mexico duty-free under NAFTA if they qualify under the rules of the agreement.

c.   Members of the European Union apply the EU common external tariff to goods from non-EU countries.

Author Contact Information

Michaela D. Platzer
Specialist in Industrial Organization and Business
mplatzer@crs.loc.gov, 7-5037

Acknowledgments

CRS specialists Cathi Jones and Michael Martin helped to shape this report by providing significant input on rules of origin and textile trade with Vietnam, respectively.